This book can be tokenized. Scan the code to claim the digital token.

T0022937

For Mom, who opened her home and heart to a rescue rooster and his human.

From an abandoned chick wandering a NYC street, to social media sensation, Bree, the Rescue Rooster, has touched many lives along his journey.

Bree and Me

A True Story of a Rescue Rooster's Journey

Story by Camille Licate

Art by Lauren Foster-MacLeod

Scan this QR code with your phone camera
for more titles from imagine and wonder

Your guarantee of quality
As publishers, we strive to produce every book to the highest commercial standards.
The printing and binding have been planned to ensure a sturdy, attractive publication
which should give years of enjoyment. If your copy fails to meet our high standards,
please inform us and we will give gladly replace it. admine@imagineandwonder.com

© Copyright 2022 Imagine & Wonder Publishers, New York
by Camille Licate, Bree and Me Rooster
ISBN: 9781637610121 (Hardcover)
Library of Congress Control Number: 2021944443

Printed in China by Hung Hing Off-set Printing Co. Ltd.

Bree was a tiny baby bird who was lost on the streets of New York City.

A kind person took Bree to an animal hospital in New York City, called Wild Bird Fund. To everyone's surprise, Bree was not a wild bird! Bree was a baby chicken! But, was Bree a boy or girl chicken?

It is hard to tell if baby chickens, called chicks, are girls or boys. A girl chicken is called a hen. A boy chicken is called a rooster.

Bree was so tiny and frightened!
Bree peeped and peeped,
calling for Mom.

PEEP!
PEEP!
PEEP!
PEEP!

But, Bree's real Mom was gone.

A young woman from Wild Bird Fund,
named Camille, knew
Bree needed to feel safe and loved.

She scooped Bree into the
palm of her hand and
held the chick close.
Bree knew everything
was going to be okay.

Camille took Bree to her tiny New York City apartment and became Bree's Foster Mom.

She would care for the little chick until he or she was old enough to go to an animal sanctuary.

Bree had a big appetite for such a little chicken.

Bree's favorite place to sleep was snuggled in Camille's pocket, where it was toasty warm.

Bree traveled everywhere with Camille, in a backpack made especially for birds.

Bree rode in cabs.

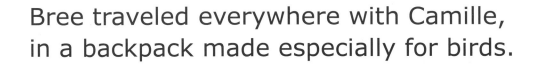

Bree rode on the subway.

Bree even rode on an airplane!

One time, the plane was delayed, and Bree spent the night in an airport hotel and ordered room service!

Bree was an awesome helper,
sorting pages and
writing emails.

Once, Bree fell fast asleep on
the warm computer keyboard.
After all, Bree was still a baby.

Bree was growing very quickly, changing every day.

Bree's yellow feathers grew into white feathers.

COMB

Bree's comb and wattle started to grow and change color.

Bree started to make a sound every morning.

WATTLE

"Cock-aw-doodwah-cwoo-crahh-doo!"

It was the strangest sound ever.

A chicken's voice changes as he or she grows.

Camille worried that Bree was a rooster.
She knew roosters were not allowed to
live in New York City. She read books
and called friends to learn about the
differences between hens and roosters.

Hens lay eggs and make a clucking sound.
Roosters protect their hens from predators and make a loud
sound called a crow.

Bree continued to grow and try new things.

Bree tried riding a bike and explored the garden.

Bree loved to cuddle with Camille every day.

Bree grew and grew and eventually, needed a medium-sized backpack.

Bree was old enough to stay home alone.
Each day, when Camille came home from work,
Bree would jump on the sofa and curl up next to her,
just like a cat or dog.

One morning Bree woke up very early.
The sun was barely in the sky.

Bree's neck extended...
Bree's beak opened wide and...
Bree crowed, "Wake up!"

"COCK-A-DOODLE-DOO!"

Camille took a deep breath.
There was no denying it.
Bree was a rooster.

Bree was surprised at his newly found voice!
His crow was REALLY LOUD!
It was so loud that the entire apartment
building heard it.
The dog outside heard it.
The birds in the trees heard it.
Even the man across the street heard it.

Camille discovered very quickly that a rooster's crow is very loud.

COCK-A-DOODLE-DOO!

COCK-A-DOODLE-DOO!

COCK-A-DOODLE-DOO!

Roosters crow early in the morning to say, "Wake up, it's a new day!"
Roosters crow throughout the day, too.
It's one way they communicate.

Is a rooster's crow as loud as a jackhammer? No.

Is it as loud as some barking dogs? No.

Is it as loud as some car horns? No.

But since it is loud, roosters are not permitted to live in New York City.

But, here they were, Bree and his Foster Mom,
Camille, living in New York City!
Bree needed a forever home outside the city
and there wasn't much time.

None of the animal sanctuaries Camille called could take a new rooster. They simply had too many rescue roosters.

ANIMAL SANCTUARIES

- Rooster Rescue — NO ROOM
- Chicken Kindness — NO ROOM
- Live Love — NO ROOM
- Feathered Friends — NO ROOM

Bree had nowhere to go.

One morning, Bree jumped into Camille's lap
and gazed at her with his big, loving eyes.
Camille knew in her heart that she could no longer
be Bree's Foster Mom. She decided to adopt
Bree and give him the forever home he deserved.

Bree and his new Mom, Camille, packed their bags,
and together, moved out of New York City
to a small town where roosters are welcome.

Bree was HOME! Camille's parents, Emily and Bill,
and their three rescue pups welcomed Bree into the family.
Neighbors, children, even the mailman, fell in love with
Bree the Rescue Rooster.
They held him, petted his wattle, and liked his crow!

Bree became the talk of the town. Bree and Camille were invited to schools and events to teach people that roosters are intelligent, loving, and loyal, and just like a cat or dog, crave love.

Bree flaps his wings when he's happy and excited. Camille calls Bree's flapping, "Big Wings."

Today, Bree uses his loud crow to spread his message!
Bree crows,

"Wake Up!
Wake Up!"

Bree Kind to Yourself.
Bree Kind to Others.
Bree Kind to All Animals.
Bree Kind to the Planet.

Bree and Camille have created the "Wake Up with Bree" series to teach and inspire kids and adults to take positive action for animals, people, and the planet.

Bree and Camille still travel together
spreading Bree's message!
He now has an extra-large backpack!

Crow along with Bree...

Bree Kind to Yourself, the Planet, and All Animals, Near and Far.

Remember Bree the Rescue Rooster, Wherever You Are.

Breelieve in a better world.

Breelieve in what you, and love, can do.

Bree the Rescue Rooster
OPENING HEARTS & MINDS

To Camille's surprise, Bree would not only change her life, but the lives of countless people who, because of Bree, now realize roosters are loving, curious, intelligent, sentient beings who want what we all want - to feel safe, peaceful and loved.

Camille created "Wake Up with Bree" educational programs, for kids to share Bree's messages with the world!

Bree is also the star of the Kids for Positive Change Series, showcasing kids taking positive action for animals, people and the planet, on select PBS stations and PBS Learning Media.

Learn more at www.WakeUpwithBree.com

Follow Bree on Instagram: @BreeandMeRooster

Meet the Author *and* Bree

Camille Licate

Camille Licate is the founder of Kids for Positive Change, an educational company empowering kids to take positive action for animals, people and the planet. She writes, hosts and produces the Kids for Positive Change television series, featured on PBS and PBS Learning Media, with Bree, the rescue rooster, by her side. Camille's three favorite things: airport reunions, vegan donuts, spending time with Bree.

Bree, the Rescue Rooster

From an abandoned chick on a New York City street to social media sensation, Bree, the rescue rooster is featured as the guest "beaker" in Camille's Wake Up with Bree educational programs. Bree's three favorite things: bird watching, blueberries, cuddles.

Meet Lauren Foster-MacLeod

Lauren has been creating art ever since she picked up her first crayon. She lives in Ottawa, Ontario, Canada where she pursues freelance art and illustration. Lauren's three favorite things: cats, singing with friends and drawing life around her.

RESOURCES

Animal sanctuaries dedicated to rescuing roosters

Rooster Haus Rescue: https://roosterhaus.org

Institute for Animal Happiness: http://www.instituteforanimalhappiness.com

Rooster Redemption: https://www.roosterredemption.org

An animal sanctuary is a safe and loving forever home for abandoned or abused animals.

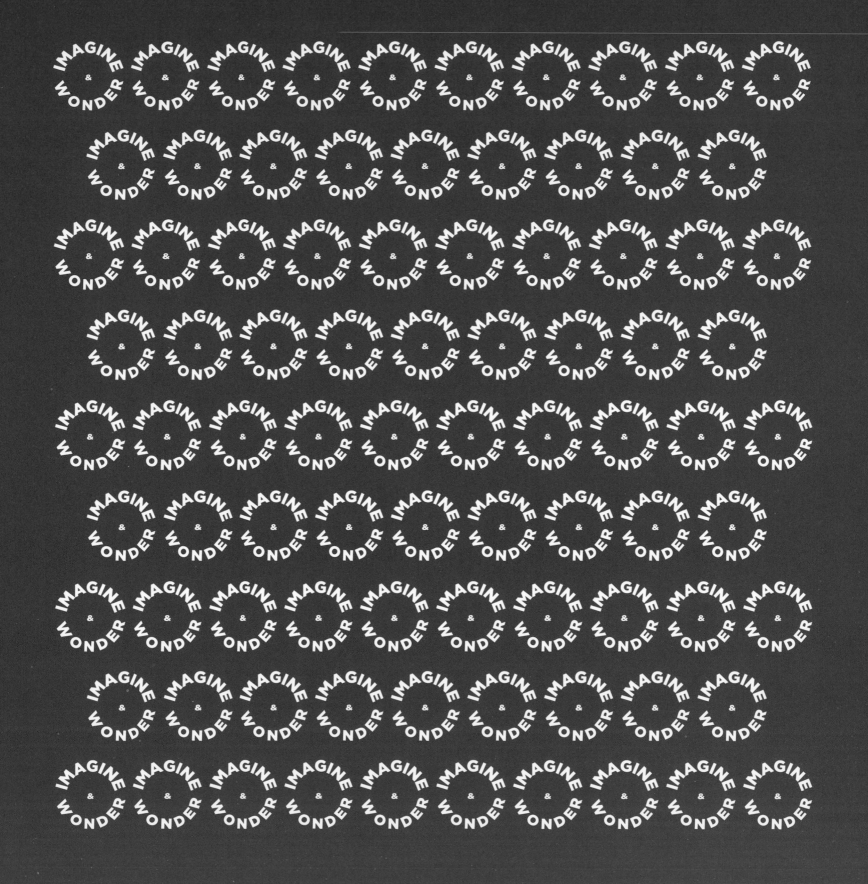